SWU-NAP- 001

UNIFORMS OF EUROPEAN ARMIES DURING THE BATAVIAN REVOLUTION

From the Amsterdam Civic Guard
to foreign armies: French, Prussian,
English, Austrian, Dutch and German states
in the years 1780-1797

SOLDIERSHOP PUBLISHING

ACKNOWLEDGEMENTS

A Special Thanks to the several institution, library, bibliotecks & athenaeums that with their good copyright policy allows us the use of many images present in this book. We remember same of this great Institutions: New York Public Library, Rara CH, Heidelberg Biblioteck University, US Library of Congress, Riikmuseum of Amsterdam, Dusseldorf University Library, Polona Library, Herzog August Bibliothek of Wolfenbüttel and many others...

Title: **UNIFORMS OF EUROPEAN ARMIES DURING THE BATAVIAN REVOLUTION**
From the Amsterdam Civic Guard to foreign armies: French, Dutch, English, Austrian, Prussian and German states in the years 1780-1797

ISBN code: 978-88-93272216 First edition March 2017

Cover & Art Design: Luca S. Cristini.

Published by Soldiershop publishing, via Padre Davide, 7 - 24050 Zanica (BG) ITALY. www.soldiershop.com

UNIFORMS OF EUROPEAN ARMIES
DURING THE BATAVIAN REVOLUTION

FROM THE AMSTERDAM CIVIC GUARD TO FOREIGN ARMIES: FRENCH, DUTCH, ENGLISH, AUSTRIAN, PRUSSIAN AND GERMAN STATES IN THE YEARS 1780-1797

With an appendix of 1799-1806, seventeen plates uniforms

Flags of Batavian Republic 1795-1806

HISTORICAL DESCRIPTION OF THE CLOTHING AND ARMS
OF THE SOLDIERS OF THE BATAVIAN REVOLUTION

Soldiershop present in this book two rare and fine collections of Dutch military print. The first series was realized by S.G. Casten, and it is dedicated to the uniforms and weapons during the Batavian Revolution, from 1787 to 1795.

The second small collection is a beautiful work of the great Dutch draughtsman, painter and etcher Jan Hendrik Langendijk related to the soldiers of Batavian Republic in 1806.

Our reprint in based on the original copy preserved in the Amsterdam Rijksmuseum. In our volume you may find the 79 plates for the first part with the missing number of 44, 46 and 47.
The second series is based on the 17 engraving of Jan Dirk Langendijk with uniforms of the "French era" of Batavian Republic in the years 1799-1806.

*

Jan Dirk Langendijk (Rotterdam, 8 March 1748 – Rotterdam, 15 December 1805) was a famous Dutch draughtsman, painter and etcher. He produced mainly depictions of land and sea battles and other military scenes from the *Dutch Patriottentijd* (circa 1780–1800) and the French Revolutionary and Napoleonic Wars (from 1792).

Born on the Bierhaven quay in the port of Rotterdam, he was the son of Hendrik Langendijk, who had come to Rotterdam from the village of Wijhe in Overijssel, and had been appointed as garbuleur by the Rotterdam chamber of the Dutch East India Company in 1772. Langendijk learned his trade from Dirck Anthonie Bisschop (1708–58), a painter of interiors, coats of arms and coaches.
He died in 1805, at a relatively young age. As an artist, Langendijk quickly focused on military scenes, evidenced by his early sketches of horses and soldiers (1769–1777).
He almost never portraited individuals but almost exclusively depicted groups, especially soldiers, officers, and horses. He was much admired in his day for his depictions of horses in battle, and a number of contemporary artists copied his work.

CONTENTS

THE BATAVIAN REVOLUTION

The "age of the democratic revolution" in the Dutch Republic culminated in two revolutions : the aborted Patriot Revolution of 1787 and the more successful Batavian Revolution of 1795 (*De Bataafse Revolutie*). For the United Provinces that age had begun after a series of crises in 1747 and resulted in the un precedented establishment of a single individual in the office of chief executive in all of the component provinces. The new form which emerged from the foreign and domestic threats of midcentury was that of a hereditary Stadhouder in the House of Orange. That family had served the Dutch state in varying capacities and with disparate consequences from its inception in the Revolt of the sixteenth century, through the triumphs of the Golden Era, to the less glorious days of the Periwig Period. The accession of William IV in 1747, his early death followed by a lengthy regency from 1752, and the accession of his son, William V, as "eminent head" of each province and chief officer of the Generality in 1766, all brought forth renewed scrutiny of the family and the offices of the Princes of Orange in the political life of the Republic. Those who were most critical of the new powers of the Stadhouderate and most desirous of reducing the dangers they saw threatening the state from the aggrandizement of that office, came to usurp the nearly exclusive use of the hoary title of Patriot.

By the end of the 18th century, the Netherlands found themselves in a deep economic crisis, caused by the devastating Fourth Anglo-Dutch War. Like in much of Europe, the people of the

The parade of the Dutch Freikorp at Sneek (Netherlands)

Lieutenant-colonel C.R.T. Krayenhoff taking his leave of General Daendels on his departure from Maarssen to Amsterdam to overthrow the Amsterdam council, 18 January 1795. Paint by Adriaan de Lelie (1755–1820)

Netherlands grew increasingly discontent with the authoritarian regime of the stadtholder, William V. During this time, the banks of the Dutch Republic held much of the world's capital. The government sponsored banks owned up a great part of Great Britain's national debt. This concentration of wealth (and the connections the government had to the House of Stuart) led to the formation of the Dutch Patriots by a minor Dutch noble named Joan van der Capellen tot den Pol. They were seeking to reduce the amount of power held by the stadtholder.

Thus, the division emerged between the Orangists, who supported the stadtholder, and the Patriots who, inspired by the ideals of the Enlightenment, desired a more democratic government and a more equal society. The Patriots built support from most of the middle-class, and founded militias (*Exercitiegenootschappen*) of armed civilians, which between 1783 and 1787 managed to take over several cities and regions in an effort to force new elections which would oust the old government officials. The Patriots held Holland and the city of Utrecht, while the Orangists held the states of Guelders and Utrecht (without the capital city).

In 1785, stadtholder William V fled his palace in the west of the country for Nijmegen in the east, as the States of Holland were not willing to send their troops to fight the Patriots. In May 1787, the stadholder's troops were defeated by the militia of Utrecht near Vreeswijk. When Princess Wilhelmina was stopped by patriot militia near Goejanverwellesluis on June 28, 1787, she applied to her brother Frederick William II of Prussia for help. On September 13 a Prussian army of 20.000 men under the command of Duke of Brunswick crossed the border. The fortress of Vianen was deserted, the city of Utrecht opened its gates. At the fortress of Woerden preparations for defense were made, but actually there was no resistance when the Prussians arrived. In Amsterdam several houses of patriot regents were plundered by mob. The stadholder returned to Gravenhage and Amsterdam, the last city to hold out, surrendered on October 10.

The Patriots continued urging citizens to resist the government by distributing pamphlets, creating "Patriot Clubs" and holding public demonstrations. The government responded by pillaging those towns where the opposition was concentrated. Most Patriots went into exile in France, while Holland's own "Ancien Régime" strengthened its grip on Dutch government chiefly through the Orangist Grand Pensionary Laurens Pieter van de Spiegel.

Batavian Republic jack (1796)

THE BATAVIAN REPUBLIC

The restoration was temporary, however. Only two years later, the French Revolution began, which embraced many of the political ideas that the Patriots had espoused in their own revolt. The Patriots enthusiastically supported the Revolution, and when the French revolutionary armies started spreading it, the Patriots joined in, hoping to liberate their own country from its authoritarian yoke. The Stadtholder joined the ill-fated First Coalition of countries in their attempt to subdue the suddenly anti-Austrian French First Republic. This War of the First Coalition also proceeded disastrously for the Stadtholder's forces, and in the severe winter of 1794/95 a French army under general Charles Pichegru, with a Dutch contingent under general Herman Willem Daendels, crossed the great frozen rivers that traditionally protected the Netherlands from invasion. Aided by the fact that a substantial proportion of the Dutch

Erection of a liberty tree on Dam Square in Amsterdam after the proclamation of the republic

Portrait of Louis Napoleon, King of Holland, Charles Howard Hodges, 1809

population looked favourably upon the French incursion, and often considered it a liberation. the French were quickly able to break the resistance of the forces of the Stadtholder, and his Austrian and British allies. However, in many cities revolution broke out even before the French arrived and Revolutionary Committees took over the city governments, and (provisionally) the national government also.

AFTERMATH

The Batavian Revolution ended with the proclamation of the Batavian Republic (*Bataafse Republiek*). It was the successor of the Republic of the Seven United Netherlands and was proclaimed on 19 January 1795. William was forced to flee to England, where he issued the Kew Letters proclaiming that all Dutch colonies were to fall under British rule, as they had declared war on the Batavian Republic. A number of these colonies, such as Sri Lanka and the Cape

In 1795 French troops invaded the Netherlands. The country became an ally of France and enjoyed a large degree of independence, until 1806 when Napoleon seized power and made his brother Louis Napoleon King of Holland. Louis showed sympathy for his new kingdom and supported Dutch interests. This had not been Napoleon's intention and in 1810 he forced his brother to abdicate. Above The increase in Amsterdam of Louis Napoleon on 20 April 1808, by Jan Anthonie Langendijk.

Colony, never returned to Dutch rule, although the Cape did so temporarily between 1803 and 1806. Several coups followed in 1798, 1801 and 1805 which brought different groups of Patriots to power. Though the French presented themselves as liberators, they behaved like conquerors. The Batavian Republic saw its end in 5 June 1806, when the Kingdom of Holland was founded, with Napoleon's brother, Louis Napoleon as King of Holland. In 1810, the area was annexed into the First French Empire, and only in 1813, the Netherlands regained their independence, with William's son, William Frederick, as sovereign prince.

English cartoon on the Dutch after the defeat of the Batavian fleet under Vice Admiral Winter against the British fleet at the Battle of Camperdown on 11 October 1797. On a throne is a pipe-smoking Dutchman dressed in a royal robe, around a group of men to the table collected. All are outraged about the bad news of the defeat brought into the battle by a messenger. In the background, a Frenchman takes some snuff from a box. On the table are two documents: a map of France with Holland as 'Department 85' and a plan for the invasion of England and reconquest of lost colonies.

NOTE ON COLOR PLATES

Sketchbook with colored drawings of the uniforms of soldiers and members of the Dutch militia and foreign armies from the period 1770 to 1795 to 1796. Realized by S.G.Gasten

1 - Uniforms of the Amsterdam civic guard from 1770-1783,
The uniform of a captain, lieutenant, sergeant and gunner of the old Amsterdam militia. Part of the chapter on the old Amsterdam militia from 1770 to 1783.

2 - Uniforms of the Amsterdam civic guard from 1770-1783,
The uniform of a lieutenant and a sergeant of the Amsterdam civic guard. Part of the chapter on the old Amsterdam militia from 1770 to 1783.

3 - Uniforms drums of the Amsterdam civic guard from 1770-1783,
The uniforms of three drums of the Amsterdam civic guard. Part of the chapter on the old Amsterdam militia from 1770 to 1783.

4 - Weapon of the Amsterdam civic guard from 1770-1783,
The coat of arms of the Amsterdam civic guard. Trophy of arms and banners, hanging from a bow. Part of the chapter on the old Amsterdam militia from 1770 to 1783.

5 - Uniforms of the Amsterdam militia in 1783-1795
The uniform of a lieutenant, drum and shooter Auxiliary of the new Amsterdam militia. Part of the second chapter on the new Amsterdam militia between 1783-1787.

6 - Uniforms of the Amsterdam militia in 1783-1795
Sergeant uniforms, grenadier and civilian shooter Auxiliary of the new Amsterdam militia. Part of the second chapter on the new Amsterdam militia between 1783-1787.

7 - Uniforms of the Amsterdam association exercise in 1783-1787,
The Grenadier Sergeant uniforms, civilian grenadier and citizen musketeer of the Amsterdam association exercise. Part of the second chapter on the new Amsterdam militia between 1783-1787.

8 - Three uniforms from the Amsterdam association exercise in 1783-1787,
The page with text about four gun-men does not correlate with the page with a representation of three members of the Amsterdam association exercise. Here's leaf torn from the album. Part of the second chapter on the new Amsterdam militia between 1783-1787.

9 - Musicians of the Amsterdam association exercise in 1783-1787,
The uniforms of musicians of the Amsterdam association exercise. Part of the second chapter on the new Amsterdam militia between 1783-1787.

10 - Musicians of the Amsterdam association exercise in 1783-1787,
The uniforms of musicians of the Amsterdam association exercise. Musicians with horn, trumpet and bassoon. Part of the second chapter on the new Amsterdam militia between 1783-1787.

11 - Constables or gunners of the Amsterdam association exercise in 1783-1787,
The uniforms of constables or gunners of the Amsterdam association exercise. Part of the second chapter on the new Amsterdam militia between 1783-1787.

12 - Uniform Cavalry of the Amsterdam association exercise in 1785-1795
The first uniform of the cavalry of the Amsterdam association exercise. Part of the second chapter on the new Amsterdam militia between 1783-1787.

13 - Uniform Cavalry of the Amsterdam association exercise in 1785-1795
The new uniform of the cavalry of the Amsterdam association exercise. Part of the second chapter on the new Amsterdam militia between 1783-1787

14 - Uniform Cavalry of the Amsterdam association exercise 1787-1795
The new uniform of the cavalry of the Amsterdam association exercise. Part of the second chapter on the new Amsterdam militia between 1783-1787.

First pages of the album in Dutch and French language and note in a colored cartouche.

- 15 Hussar of the Rhine Count of Salm in 1786-1795

The uniform of the Hussars of the Rhine Count of Salm in 1786. Part of the second chapter on the new uniforms for the period 1783-1787.

16 - Hussar of the Rhine Count of Salm in 1786-1795

The uniform of the cuirassiers of the Rhine Count of Salm in 1786. Part of the second chapter on the new uniforms for the period 1783-1787.

17 - Uniforms of the corps of the Rhine Count of Salm in 1786-1795

The uniform of the riflemen, scoop shooters and hunters of the Rhine Count of Salm in 1786. Part of the second chapter on the new uniforms for the period 1783-1787.

18 - Uniforms of soldiers in the Defence Being and the Utrecht garrison in 1786-1795

The uniform of military personnel in the Defence Being and the Utrecht garrison in 1786. Part of the second chapter on the new uniforms for the period 1783-1787.

19 - Uniform of a cavalryman of Hope Regiment, 1795

The page with text about the ulaan does not correlate with the page with the representation of a rider Regiment of Hope in the service of the Defense Commission. Here's leaf torn from the album. Part of the second chapter on the new uniforms for the period 1783-1787.

20 - Uniform of a Famas cavalryman, 1795

The uniform of a Famas cavalryman. Part of the second chapter on the new uniforms for the period 1783-1787.

21 - Different uniform of 1786-1795

The uniform of a hulan, hussar, cuirassier, gunner and a musketeer of Palardie (Palardy) in 1786. Part of the second chapter on the new uniforms for the period 1783-1787.

22 - Uniforms of the crew of the battery on the Amstel River in 1787-1795

The uniform of an officer, gunner, carpenter and worth Gelder on the floating battery patriots on the Amstel River in 1787. Part of the second chapter on the new uniforms for the period 1783-1787.

23A - Title for the third chapter on the new uniforms after the arrival of the Prussian troops in 1787, 1795 – 1796 Colored cartouche with the title for the third chapter on the new uniforms in the period after the restoration of the Prince of Orange and the arrival of the Prussian troops in Holland in 1787. (at pag. 28)

23B - Arm Trophy Amsterdam 1787-1795

Arm Trophy in restoring the governor William V in 1787. Part of the third chapter on the new uniforms in the period after the restoration of the Prince of Orange and the arrival of the Prussian troops in Holland in 1787.

24 - Uniforms of the Amsterdam association exercise in 1787,
The uniforms of citizens of the Amsterdam association exercise. Part of the third chapter on the new uniforms in the period after the restoration of the Prince of Orange and the arrival of

25 - uniforms of the Prussian Marwits Regiment in 1787,
The uniforms of soldiers of the Prussian Marwits Regiment. Part of the third chapter on the new uniforms in the period after the restoration of the Prince of Orange and the arrival of the Prussian troops in Holland in 1787.

26 - Uniforms of civilians in sadness by the arrival of the Prussians in 1787,
The uniforms of civilians in anticipation of the arrival of the Prussian troops. Part of the third chapter on the new uniforms in the period after the restoration of the Prince of Orange and the arrival of the Prussian troops in Holland in 1787.

27 - Uniforms of Prussian officers,
The uniforms of three Prussian officers. Part of the third chapter on the new uniforms in the period after the restoration of the Prince of Orange and the arrival of the Prussian troops in Holland in 1787.

28 - Uniforms of Prussian soldiers,
The uniforms of four Prussian soldiers: two musketeers, grenadier and fusilier. Part of the third chapter on the new uniforms in the period after the restoration of the Prince of Orange and the arrival of the Prussian troops in Holland in 1787.

29 - Uniforms of the Prussian cavalry,
The Prussian cavalry uniforms: blue Hussar, black hussar, dragoon, cuirassier and cuirassier of Kalkreuth. Part of the third chapter on the new uniforms in the period after the restoration of the Prince of Orange and the arrival of the Prussian troops in Holland in 1787.

30 - Uniforms of the Dutch Guards in Amsterdam,   1795 -1796
The uniforms of two Dutch Gardes in Amsterdam in 1787. Part of the third chapter on the new uniforms in the period after the restoration of the Prince of Orange and the arrival of the Prussian troops in Holland in 1787.

31 - Prussian cavalry in Amsterdam,
The uniforms of two Prussian cavalry in Amsterdam in 1787. Part of the third chapter on the new uniforms in the period after the restoration of the Prince of Orange and the arrival of the Prussian troops in Holland in 1787.

32 - Six Prussian soldiers,
The uniforms of six Prussian soldiers: dragoon, two gunners, hunter and an officer of the regiment Marwits. Part of the third chapter on the new uniforms in the period after the restoration of the Prince of Orange and the arrival of the Prussian troops in Holland in 1787.

33 - First troops in Amsterdam in 1787,

The uniforms of the first troops arrived in Amsterdam in 1787: Suisses of May and troops of Orange-Nassau. Part of the third chapter on the new uniforms in the period after the restoration of the Prince of Orange and the arrival of the Prussian troops in Holland in 1787.

34 - Uniforms of the new Amsterdam militia in 1787,

Five uniforms of the new Amsterdam militia in 1787: an officer, sergeant, corporal, ordinary citizens or shooter and a drummer. Part of the third chapter on the new uniforms in the period after the restoration of the Prince of Orange and the arrival of the Prussian troops in Holland in 1787.

35 - Uniforms of grenadiers and the Crown Prince of Orange-Nassau in 1788,   1795 – 1796

Three uniforms of grenadiers of the Crown Prince and Orange-Nassau in 1788: grenadier corporal and a grenadier of the hereditary prince and an ordinary grenadier of Orange-Nassau. Part of the third chapter on the new uniforms in the period after the restoration of the Prince of Orange and the arrival of the Prussian troops in Holland in 1787.

36 - Uniforms of grenadiers and musketeer,

Four uniforms of grenadiers of Orange and Nassau, Westerloo and the hereditary prince and a musketeer of Waldeck, 1788. Part of the third chapter on the new uniforms in the period after the restoration of the Prince of Orange and the arrival of the Prussian troops Holland in 1787.

37 - Uniform of a Van Cat cavalryman,

The uniform of a Van Poes cavalry regiment, 1788. Part of the third chapter on the new uniforms in the period after the restoration of the Prince of Orange and the arrival of the Prussian troops in Holland in 1787.

38 - Uniforms of the Gardes,

Uniforms of the Gardes Dragons and the Dutch Guards, 1788. Part of the third chapter on the new uniforms in the period after the restoration of the Prince of Orange and the arrival of the Prussian troops in Holland in 1787.

39 - Uniforms of the Gardes and Hussar,

Uniforms of three riders: Dutch Gardes Dragons, Dutch Gardes and a hussar Van Eeker, 1788. Part of the third chapter on the new uniforms in the period after the restoration of the Prince of Orange and the arrival of the Prussian troops in Holland 1787.

40 - Uniforms of Grenadiers and Musketeers,

Uniforms of two grenadiers and two musketeers of the Swiss and the Dutch Guards, 1788. Part of the third chapter on the new uniforms in the period after the restoration of the Prince of Orange and the arrival of the Prussian troops in Holland in 1787.

41 - Uniforms Musketeers,
Uniforms of four musketeers, 1788. The page with text about six uniforms does not correlate with the page with the presentation of four soladten. Here's leaf torn from the album. Part of the third chapter on the new uniforms in the period after the restoration of the Prince of Orange and the arrival of the Prussian troops in Holland in 1787.

42 - Uniforms of Grenadiers and Musketeers,
Uniforms of two Grenadiers Regiment Walloons and Bijlandt and Puttoo and two musketeers of Mecklenburg troops and Westerloo, 1788. Part of the third chapter on the new uniforms in the period after the restoration of the Prince of Orange and the arrival of the Prussian in 1787.

43 - Uniforms of Mecklenburg and Waldeck,
Five different uniforms of a corporal grenadier and musketeer of the Mecklenburg troops and two musketeers and a hunter Regiment Waldeck, 1788. Part of the third chapter on the new uniforms in the period after the restoration of the Prince of Orange and the arrival of the Prussian in 1787.

44 - Missing plates

45 - uniform of a hussar of Van Eeker,
The uniform of a hussar of Van Eeker (with mantle?), 1788. The page with text may not correlate with the opposite page with the performance. Possibly a leaf torn from the album here. Part of the third chapter on the new uniforms in the period after the restoration of the Prince of Orange and the arrival of the Prussian troops in Holland in 1787.

46 - Missing plates

47 - Missing plates

48 - Six different uniforms,
Various uniforms of foreign regiments, ca. 1788-1795. The page with text does not correlate with the opposite page with the performance. Here is a leaf torn from the album. Part of the third chapter on the new uniforms in the period after the restoration of the Prince of Orange and the arrival of the Prussian troops in Holland in 1787.

49 - Different uniforms,
Six soldiers from a likely foreign infantry regiment, ca. 1788-1795. The page with text does not correlate with the opposite page with the performance. Here is a leaf torn from the album. Part of the third chapter on the new uniforms in the period after the restoration of the Prince of Orange and the arrival of the Prussian troops in Holland in 1787.

50 - Different uniforms of British Rangers,
Six uniform of an English regiment Rangers, ca. 1788-1795. Officer, drum major, hunters, musicians and a sergeant gunner in English service. Part of the third chapter on the new uniforms in the period after the restoration of the Prince of Orange and the arrival of the Prussian in 1787.

51 - Uniforms of musicians of the Rangers,
Uniforms of five musicians in the expatriate English regiment of Rangers, ca. 1788-1795. Drum major, two drummers, a piper and musician. Part of the third chapter on the new uniforms in the period after the restoration of the Prince of Orange and the arrival of the Prussian in 1787.

52 - Uniforms of British grenadiers and musketeers,
Uniforms of four British grenadiers and musketeers, ca. 1788-1795. Part of the third chapter on the new uniforms in the period after the restoration of the Prince of Orange and the arrival of the Prussian troops in Holland in 1787.

53 - Uniforms of British soldiers,
Uniforms of four British soldiers, ca. 1788-1795. Two musketeers, one of the Rangers geewone hunter and a hunter. Part of the third chapter on the new uniforms in the period after the restoration of the Prince of Orange and the arrival of the Prussian troops in Holland in 1787.

54 - Uniform of a Dutch carabiner,
Uniform of a Dutch carabiner horseback, ca. 1788-1795. Part of the third chapter on the new uniforms in the period after the restoration of the Prince of Orange and the arrival of the Prussian troops in Holland in 1787.

55 - Uniforms of English cavalry,
The uniforms of four British cavalrymen, ca. 1788-1795. The page with the text does not correlate with the page with the performance. Here's leaf torn from the album. Part of the third chapter on the new uniforms in the period after the restoration of the Prince of Orange and the arrival of the Prussian troops in Holland in 1787.

56 - Uniforms of French cavalry of Conde regiment,
The uniforms of two French cavalrymen of the emigrant regiment of Conde, ca. 1788-1795. Part of the third chapter on the new uniforms in the period after the restoration of the Prince of Orange and the arrival of the Prussian troops in Holland in 1787.

57 - Uniforms of French cavalry of Rohan,
The uniforms of two French cavalrymen of the French Emigrants, Corps of the Prince of Rohan, ca. 1788-1795. Part of the third chapter on the new uniforms in the period after the restoration of the Prince of Orange and the arrival of the Prussian troops in Holland in 1787.

58 - Uniforms of English cavalry,
The uniforms of three British cavalrymen, ca. 1788-1795. An English hunter horse, rider and hussar. Part of the third chapter on the new uniforms in the period after the restoration of the Prince of Orange and the arrival of the Prussian troops in Holland in 1787.

59 - Uniform of English cavalry,
The uniform of a British cavalryman, ca. 1788-1795. Part of the third chapter on the new uniforms in the period after the restoration of the Prince of Orange and the arrival of the Prussian in 1787.

60 - Uniform of English cavalry,
The uniform of two British cavalrymen, ca. 1788-1795. Part of the third chapter on the new uniforms in the period after the restoration of the Prince of Orange and the arrival of the Prussian troops in Holland in 1787.

61 - Uniform of English hussar,
The uniform of an English hussar, ca. 1788-1795. Part of the third chapter on the new uniforms in the period after the restoration of the Prince of Orange and the arrival of the Prussian in 1787.

62 - Uniform of English hussar,
The uniform of an English hussar, ca. 1788-1795. Part of the third chapter on the new uniforms in the period after the restoration of the Prince of Orange and the arrival of the Prussian in 1787.

63 - Uniform of English cavalryman,
The uniform of a British cavalryman, ca. 1788-1795. Part of the third chapter on the new uniforms in the period after the restoration of the Prince of Orange and the arrival of the Prussian troops in Holland in 1787.

64 - Uniform of Scottish soldiers,
The uniform of two Scottish soldiers, ca. 1788-1795. Part of the third chapter on the new uniforms in the period after the restoration of the Prince of Orange and the arrival of the Prussian troops in Holland in 1787.

65 - Uniform troops of Hanover,
The uniform of an officer and a musketeer of the troops of Hanover, ca. 1788-1795. Part of the third chapter on the new uniforms in the period after the restoration of the Prince of Orange and the arrival of the Prussian troops in Holland in 1787.

66 - Uniform of English troops, 1796
The uniforms of two English Gardes and a grenadier, ca. 1788-1795. Part of the third chapter on the new uniforms in the period after the restoration of the Prince of Orange and the arrival of the Prussian troops in Holland in 1787.

67 - Uniforms of English jagers,
The uniforms of a group of English chasseur at their post, a group of soldiers in the distance, ca. 1788-1795. Part of the third chapter on the new uniforms in the period after the restoration of the Prince of Orange and the arrival of the Prussian troops in Holland in 1787.

68 - Uniform of English hussar,
The uniform of a British Hussar on horseback who are present in the field, ca. 1788-1795. The page with the text does not correlate with the page with the performance. Here's leaf torn from the album. Part of the third chapter on the new uniforms in the period after the restoration of the Prince of Orange and the arrival of the Prussian troops in Holland in 1787.

69 - Uniform of English hussar,

The uniform of a British Hussar on horseback who gefourageerd in the field, ca. 1788-1795. Part of the third chapter on the new uniforms in the period after the restoration of the Prince of Orange and the arrival of the Prussian troops in Holland in 1787.

70 - Uniform of English hussar,

The uniform of a British Hussar on horseback who gefourageerd in the field, ca. 1788-1795. Part of the third chapter on the new uniforms in the period after the restoration of the Prince of Orange and the arrival of the Prussian troops in Holland in 1787.

71 - Uniform of Dutch and French hussars,

The uniforms of two huzeren Regiment der Hoop and two hussars French Emigrants, ca. 1788-1795. Part of the third chapter on the new uniforms in the period after the restoration of the Prince of Orange and the arrival of the Prussian troops in Holland in 1787.

72 - Uniform of hussars of Prince Rohan regiment,

The uniforms of a patrol of French cavalrymen of the French Emigrants, Corps of the Prince of Rohan, ca. 1788-1795. Part of the third chapter on the new uniforms in the period after the restoration of the Prince of Orange and the arrival of the Prussian troops in Holland in 1787.

73 - Uniform of Imperial General,

The uniform of a general of the Austrian imperial troops, horse, ca. 1788-1795. Part of the third chapter on the new uniforms in the period after the restoration of the Prince of Orange and the arrival of the Prussian troops in Holland in 1787.

74 - Uniforms of Imperial officers,

The uniforms of two officers of the Austrian imperial troops, horse, ca. 1788-1795. The page with the text does not correlate with the page with the performance. Here's leaf torn from the album. Part of the third chapter on the new uniforms in the period after the restoration of the Prince of Orange and the arrival of the Prussian troops in Holland in 1787.

75 - Uniform of an Imperial hussar,

The uniform of a Hussar of the Austrian imperial troops, horse, ca. 1788-1795. Part of the third chapter on the new uniforms in the period after the restoration of the Prince of Orange and the arrival of the Prussian troops in Holland in 1787.

76 - Uniform of an Imperial officer,   1795

The uniform of an officer of the Austrian imperial troops, horse, ca. 1788-1795. Part of the third chapter on the new uniforms in the period after the restoration of the Prince of Orange and the arrival of the Prussian troops in Holland in 1787.

77 - Uniforms of Imperial officers,

The uniforms of three officers of the Austrian imperial troops, horse, ca. 1788-1795. Cuirassier, dragoon and constable. Part of the third chapter on the new uniforms in the period after the restoration of the Prince of Orange and the arrival of the Prussian troops in Holland in 1787.

78 - Uniforms of foreign cavalry,

The uniforms of five officers of the cavalry. Croat, Hungarian hussar, dragoon Liechtenstein, and an Austrian imperial dragoon and cuirassier, all on horseback, ca. 1788-1795. Part of the third chapter on the new uniforms in the period after the restoration of the Prince of Orange and the arrival of the Prussian troops in Holland in 1787.

79 - uniforms of Imperial artillery,

Five constables of the Austrian imperial troops, with a gun, ca. 1788-1795. Part of the third chapter on the new uniforms in the period after the restoration of the Prince of Orange and the arrival of the Prussian troops in Holland in 1787.

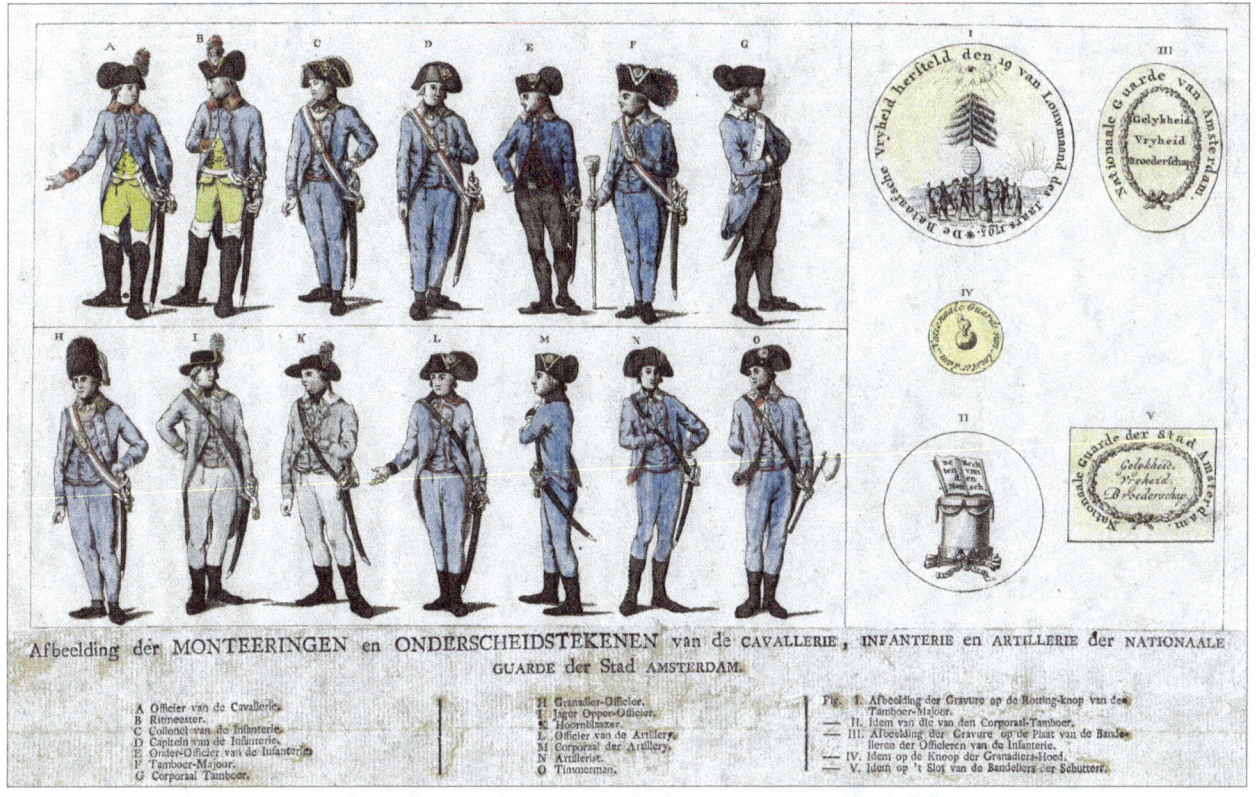

The Amsterdam militia and guard in 1795

Engraving of Batavian republic soldier (1799-1806) by Jan Dirk Langendijk

A - 1801 An officer of 1st Half Brigade of the Army Batavian, walking with a lady on his arm.

B - 1804 Grenadier officer and a soldier of the Body Guard of the Grand Pensionary of the Batavian Republic.

C - 1801 An officer of the engineers of the Batavian army, walking with a lady on his arm.

D - 1804 Batavian Colonial Infantry of the Cape of Good Hope,

E - 1804 Two soldiers of a regiment of Hussar standing,

F - 1801 Two drum major of infantry regiment standing,

G - 1804 Grenadier of the Guard of his Excellency the *Raadpensionaris*,

H - 1804 Two soldiers of an Hussar regiment standing,

I - 1804 Two soldiers with Oriental turbans,

J - 1800 Soldier drawing his saber,

K - 1801 Member of the Rotterdam armed citizen force with a rifle,

L - 1804 Soldier of infantry in campaign dress,

M - 1802 Mounted cavalryman,

N - 1799 English forces near Bergen,

O - 1787 Uniform of the Arms Trade Rotterdamsch Society of the Palm Tree,

P - 1804 Soldier, brandishing an ax,

Q - 1799 An English guardsman and a Russian grenadier, dressed in uniform in a conversation.

Capture of the Russian General Hermann at the battle of Bergen 1799

Dirk Langendijk self portrait

Het Landen

Der ENGELSCHE *, tusschen* PETTE *en* CALLANTVOOG, *op den 27 Augustus des Jaars 1799.*

Landing of British troops at Callantsoog, 1799, Cornelis Brouwer, after Jan Anthonie Langendijk

COLOUR PLATES

1st part

1780-1795

Reflextie of
Waare En Natuurlyke
afbeeldinge Van de Nieuw
Burgery, Geformeert tot
een Corps Oculaire
in 't Jaar 1783 tot 87

In Amsterdam
1795
S. G. Casten

Uniforms of the Amsterdam civic guard from 1770-1783

Uniforms of the Amsterdam civic guard from 1770-1783

Uniforms drums of the Amsterdam civic guard from 1770-1783

Weapon of the Amsterdam civic guard from 1770-1783.

Uniforms of the Amsterdam militia in 1783-1795.

Uniforms of the Amsterdam militia in 1783, 1795.

Uniforms of the Amsterdam association exercise in 1783-1787.

Three uniforms from the Amsterdam association exercise in 1783-1787.

Musicians of the Amsterdam association exercise in 1783-1787.

Musicians of the Amsterdam association exercise in 1783-1787.

Constables or gunners of the Amsterdam association exercise in 1783-1787.

Uniform Cavalry of the Amsterdam association exercise in 1785, 1795.

Uniform Cavalry of the Amsterdam association exercise in 1785, 1795.

Uniform Cavalry of the Amsterdam association exercise 1787-1795.

Hussar of the Rhine Count of Salm in 1786, 1795.

Hussar of the Rhine Count of Salm in 1786, 1795.

Uniforms of the corps of the Rhine Count of Salm in 1786, 1795.

Uniforms of soldiers in the Defence Being and the Utrecht garrison in 1786, 1795.

Uniform of a cavalryman of Hope Regiment,   1795.

uniform of a Famas cavalryman,   1795.

Different uniform of 1786, 1795.

Uniforms of the crew of the battery on the Amstel River in 1787, 1795.

Arm Trophy Amsterdam 1787 1795.

Uniforms of the Amsterdam association exercise in 1787.

Uniforms of the Prussian Marwits Regiment in 1787.

Uniforms of civilians in sadness by the arrival of the Prussians in 1787.

Uniforms of Prussian officers.

Uniforms of Prussian soldiers.

Uniforms of Prussian cavalry.

uniforms of the Dutch Guards in Amsterdam, 1795 -1796.

Prussian cavalry in Amsterdam

Six Prussian soldiers.

First troops in Amsterdam in 1787.

Uniforms of the new Amsterdam militia in 1787.

Uniforms of grenadiers and the Crown Prince of Orange-Nassau in 1788,   1795 – 1796 .

Uniforms of grenadiers and musketeer.

Uniform of a cavalryman of Van Cat regiment.

Uniforms Gardes.

Uniforms Gardes and Hussar.

Uniforms of Grenadiers and Musketeers.

Uniforms Musketeers.

Uniforms of Grenadiers and Musketeers.

Uniforms Mecklenburg and Waldeck.

Uniform of an hussar of Van Eeker. regiment

48

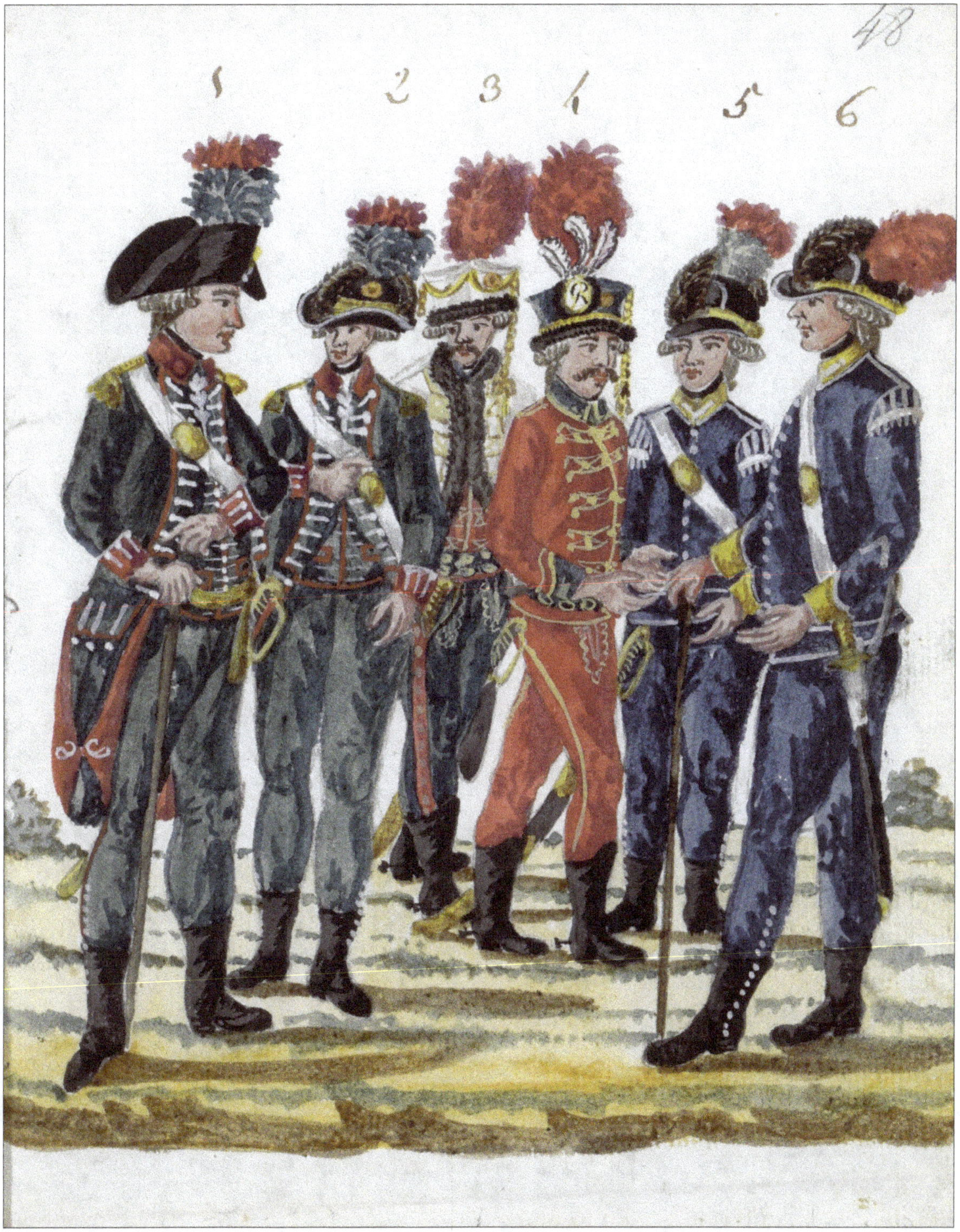

Six different uniforms.

Different British uniforms.

Different uniforms of British Rangers.

Uniforms of musicians of the Rangers.

Uniforms of British grenadiers and musketeers.

Uniforms of British soldiers.

Uniform of a Dutch carabiner.

55

Uniforms of English cavalry.

Uniforms of French cavalry of Conde regiment.

Uniforms of French cavalry of Rohan regiment.

Uniforms of English cavalry.

Uniform of English cavalry.

Uniform of English cavalry.

Uniform of English hussar.

Uniform of English hussar.

Uniform of English cavalryman.

64

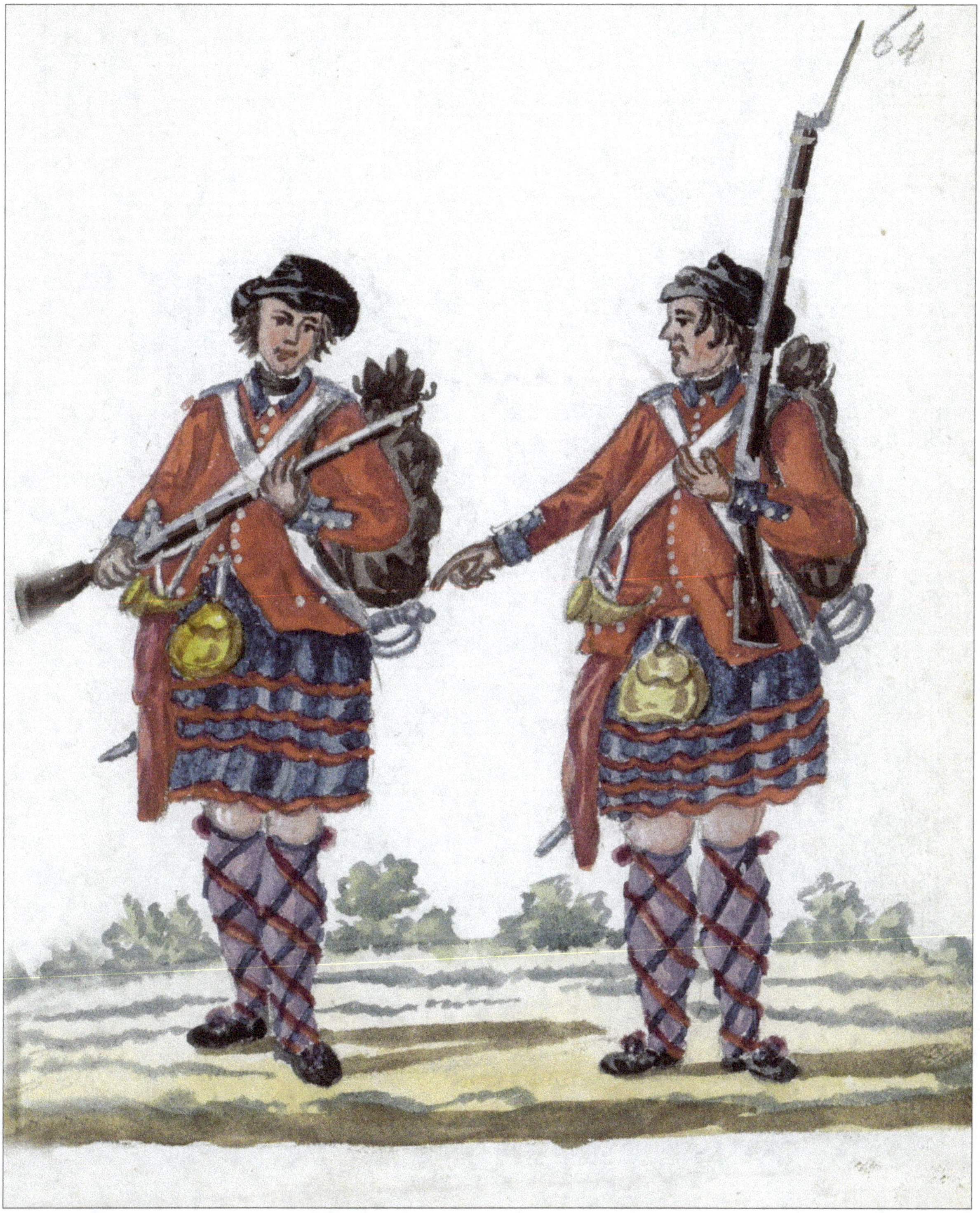

Uniform of Scottish soldiers.

Uniform troops of Hanover.

Uniform of English troops, 1796.

Uniforms of English Jagers.

Uniform of English hussar.

69

Uniform of English hussar.

Uniform of English hussar.

Uniform of Dutch and French hussars.

Uniform of hussars of Prince Rohan regiment.

Uniform of Imperial General.

Uniforms of imperial officers.

Uniform of an imperial hussar.

Uniform of an imperial officer, 1795.

Uniforms of imperial officers.

Uniforms of foreign cavalry.

Uniforms of imperial artillery.

COLOUR PLATES

2nd part

1799-1806

1801 An officer of 1st Half Brigade of the Army Batavian, walking with a lady on his arm.

1804 Grenadier officer and a soldier of the Grand Pensionary guard of the Batavian Republic.

1801 An officer of the engineers of the Batavian army, walking with a lady on his arm.

1804 Batavian Colonial Infantry of the Cape of Good Hope.

1804 Two soldiers of a regiment of Hussar standing.

1801 Two drum major of infantry regiment standing.

1804 Grenadier of the Guard of his Excellency the Raad pensionaris

1804 Two soldiers of an Hussar regiment standing.

1804 Two soldiers with Oriental turbans.

1800 Soldier drawing his saber.

1801 Member of the Rotterdam armed citizen force with a rifle.

1804 Soldier of infantry in campaign dress.

1802 Mounted cavalryman

1799 English forces near Bergen.

1787 Uniform of the Arms Trade Rotterdamsch Society of the Palm Tree

1804 Soldier, brandishing an ax.

Engelsche Gardes en Rusfiech Granadier

1799 An English guardsman and a Russian grenadier, dressed in uniform in a conversation.

BIBLIOGRAPHY

ON BATAVIAN REVOLUTION

- *Klein, S.R.E.* (1995) Patriots Republikanisme. Politieke cultuur in Nederland (1766-1787).
- *Leeb, I.L.* (1973) The Ideological Origins of the Batavian Revolution.
- *Verweij, G.* (1996) Geschiedenis van Nederland. Levensverhaal van zijn bevolking.
- *Pieter Geyl* , La Révolution batave (1783-1798), Paris, Société des études robespierristes, 1971, 386 p.
- *Jacques Godechot*, Les révolutions, 1770-1799, Paris, PUF, 1963, 441 p.
- *Jonathan Israel*, The Dutch Republic : Its Rise, Greatness, and Fall 1477-1806, Oxford, 1995.
- *Eke Poortinga*, "Fédéralisme et centralisation autour des révolutions batave et française".
- *Annie Jourdan & Joep Leerssen*, Remous révolutionnaires : République batave, armée française, Amsterdam, 1996.
- *Annie Jourdan*, La révolution Batave, entre la France et l'Amérique (1795-1806), Rennes, 2008
- *Simon Schama*, Patriots and Liberators : Revolution in the Netherlands 1780 - 1830, New York, Collins, 1977.
- *George Edmundson*, History of Holland, Cambridge University Press, 1922.

ON BATAVIAN REPUBLIC

- *Vries, J. de, and Woude, A. van der* (1997), The First Modern Economy. Success, Failure, and Perseverance of the Dutch Economy, 1500-1815, Cambridge University Press.
- *Louis Bergeon, François Furet, Reinhart Koselleck*; Historia Universal 26. La época de las Revoluciones Europeas. 1780-1848. Ed. Siglo XXI de España, 1976.
- *Blanning, T. C. W.*, The French Revolutionary Wars, 1787-1801.
- *Karl Heinrich Ludwig Pölitz:* Die europäischen Verfassungen seit 1789 bis auf die neueste Zeit, Band 2, Leipzig: F. A. Brockhaus, 1833.
- Constitutions-Acte für die Batavische Republik vom 23. April 1798.
- *Carl von Rotteck*: Allgemeine politische Annalen, Band 7, Cotta'sche Buchhandlung, 1831.
- *Wayne Te Brake*, Regents and Rebels, The Revolutionary World of an Eighteenth-Century Dutch City, Cambridge, 1989, 213 p.
- *Frans Grijzenhout*, Het Bataafse experiment: politiek en cultuur rond 1800, Vantilt uitgeverij, 2013.
- *Joost Rosendaal*, Bataven!: Nederlandse vluchtelingen in Frankrijk, 1787-1795, druk 2003
- *Joost Rosendaal*, De Nederlandse Revolutie: vrijheid, volk en vaderland, 1783-1799, druk 2005.
- *Mart Rutjes*, Door gelijkheid gegrepen: democratie, burgerschap en staat in Nederland 1795-1801, 2013.
- *Donald Sutherland*, Revolutie en contrarevolutie: Frankrijk 1789-1815, druk 1989, p. 478, Bert Bakker - Amsterdam.
- *Louis Legrand*, La Révolution française en Hollande, Paris, Hachette, 1894, 398 p.
- *Jean-Bernard Manger*, Recherches sur les relations économiques entre la France et la Hollande pendant la Révolution française (1785-1795), Paris, 1923, 170 p.
- *Arthur Elias*, "La néerlandicité de la constitution de 1798 " in Annales historiques de la Révolution française, n° 326, octobre-décembre 2001, pp. 43-52
- *Annie Jourdan*, "la république batave et le 18 brumaire " in Annales historiques de la Révolution française, n° 318, octobre-décembre 1999, pp. 755-772
- *Niek van Sas*, "L'impératif patriotique, mutation conceptuelle et conjoncture politique 1795-1813" in Annales historiques de la Révolution française, n° 326, octobre/décembre 2001, pp. 25-42

De Bataille
Van BERGEN den 19 September 1799.

SOLDIERS, WEAPONS & UNIFORMS ALREADY PUBLISHED
(TITLES ALREADY PUBLISHED)

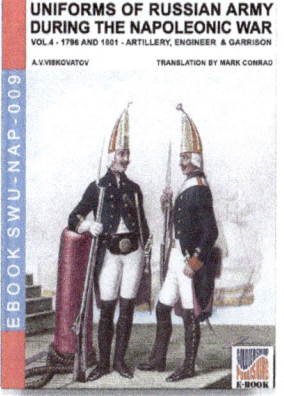

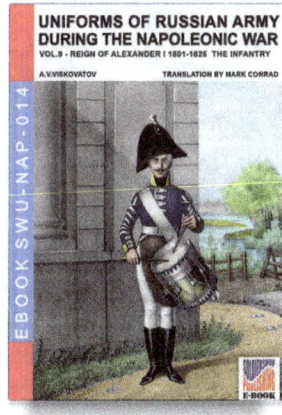